Just Handwri
Cursive Handwriting Pr

6th Class

educate.ie

Author: Mary Donnelly
Editor: Susan McKeever
Design: Philip Ryan Graphic Design
Illustration: Martin Pierce

Mr Unsworth by Roald Dahl courtesy Jonathan Cape Ltd and Penguin Books Ltd.

© 2012 Educate.ie, Castleisland, County Kerry, Ireland.

ISBN: 978-1-908507-20-4

Printed in Ireland by Walsh Colour Print, Castleisland, County Kerry. Freephone 1800 613 111.

Contents

Introduction

The **Just Handwriting** series consists of:
Just Handwriting: Early Years (3-4 years)
Just Handwriting: Early Years (4-5 years)
Just Handwriting Script: Junior Infants to Second Class. (Includes a practice copy for each class.)
Just Handwriting Cursive: Junior Infants to Sixth Class. (Includes a practice copy for each class from Junior Infants to Second Class.)

The aim of the programme is to enable children to write fluently, comfortably, quickly and legibly. Handwriting is a form of communication and one on which we are often judged.

Remember the Four Ps: Preparation, Pencil Grip, Posture, Practice.

Preparation (Junior Infants to Second Class): The simple, fun 'Let's Get Ready!' exercises help to relax the child mentally and physically and enable them to focus on the planned activity. Encourage the child to draw or trace the 'Giant Sunglasses' before every writing activity. In time, it will become part of their work routine.

Pencil Grip: The correct pencil grip will lead to quick, fluent writing.

Posture: Good posture helps the writing stamina of the child.

Practice: The formation of each letter is clearly illustrated so the child will have a reference that shows him or her how to form each letter, especially if more than one stroke is involved. Handwriting is an essential skill that needs to be taught and fluency only comes with plenty of practice. Practice, practice, practice makes perfect and enables the child to become a confident writer.

Assessment

There is a self-assessment option at the bottom of each page. The child ticks the face that they feel applies to their completion of the page.

Individual Books (Pre-cursive to Cursive Version)

Junior Infants Book: This book focuses on the correct formation of all lowercase letters. The letters are pre-cursive (with 'tails'). This level also includes a practice copy; this focuses on the formation of lowercase letters, and can be used at the teacher's discretion.

Senior Infants and First Class Books: These books focus on the correct formation of all uppercase letters as well as further practice in lowercase. Both books include a practice copy, focusing on capital letters, that can be used at the teacher's discretion.

Second Class Book: In the Second Class book the width of the lines changes from 6mm to 5mm from Page 39 onwards in preparation for third class. All writing exercises are meaningful e.g. recipes, quiz-style questions and answers and interesting facts. (Includes a practice copy.)

Third to Sixth Class (Cursive Writing)

Third Class Book: This is the stage where children are introduced to cursive looped writing. They will discover that many of the lowercase letters are unchanged from those that have been taught already. Most of the remaining letters involve loops. Later in the year the capital letters are introduced.

Fourth Class Book: Now the children begin to write using a pen. An inexpensive cartridge pen with a fine-pointed nib or a fine-pointed fibre pen (not felt) is recommended. Under no circumstances should a biro or a ballpoint pen be used. In fact these types of pens should not be used for writing in any primary school class.

The Fifth Class Book: Lower and uppercase letters are repeated from Pages 3 to 11 to revise, reinforce and provide practice of correct letter formation. The most important writing rules are repeated throughout the book. Pupils should use the same pen suggested in the Fourth Class book. The contents of this book vary from facts, stories and poetry to dictionary exercises and legends.

The Sixth Class Book: Lower and uppercase letters from Pages 3 to 8 provide revision of letter formation. Once again the writing rules are repeated throughout the book. The first half of the book has blue and red lines; the second half of the book has double blue lines for 12 pages and 'copy' lines for the last 12 pages. Pupils are recommended to use the same type of pen as they used in Fourth and Fifth Class. There is a variety of material in this book − factual pieces, legends, riddles, stories and tongue twisters.

acdeimnoq

a a a a a a a a a a a a a a a a a a a a a a a a

a a a a a a a a a a a a a a a a a a a a a

c c c c c c c c c c c c c c c c c c c c c c

c c c c c c c c c c c c c c c c c c

d d d d d d d d d d d d d d d d d d d d d d d

d d d d d d d d d d d d d d d d d d d d

e e e e e e e e e e e e e e e e e e e e e e e e

e e e e e e e e e e e e e e e e e e e e e

i i i i i i i i i i i i i i i i i i i i i i

i i i i i i i i i i i i i i i i i i i i i

m m m m m m m m m m m m m m m m m m m m m m

m m m m m m m m m m m m m m m m m m m m

n n n n n n n n n n n n n n n n n n n n n n

n n n n n n n n n n n n n n n n n n n n

o o o o o o o o o o o o o o o o o o o o o o o

o o o o o o o o o o o o o o o o o o o o o o

q q q q q q q q q q q q q q q q q q q q q q

q q q q q q q q q q q q q q q q q q q q q q

q q q q q q q q q q q q q q q q q q q q q q

☹ ☐ 😐 ☐ ☺ ☐

3

t u v x h k l b j g

Checklist
Sit up straight ☐
Don't grip your pen too tightly ☐
Keep your writing forearm on the desk ☐

t t t t t t t t t t t t t t t t t t t t t t
t t t t t t t t t t t t t t t t t t t t t

u u u u u u u u u u u u u u u u u u u u u u u
u

x x x x x x x x x x x x x x x x x x x x x x
x x x x x x x x x x x x x x x x x x x x x x

h h h h h h h h h h h h h h h h h h h h h h h
h h h h h h h h h h h h h h h h h h h h h

k k k k k k k k k k k k k k k k k k k k k k k
k k k k k k k k k k k k k k k k k k k k k

l l l l l l l l l l l l l l l l l l l l l l l l
l l l l l l ll l l ll l l l l ll

b b b b b b b b b b b b b b b b b b b b b b
b b b b b b b b b b b b b b b b b b b b b b

j j j j j j j j j j j j j j j j j j j j j j j
j j j j j j j j j j j j j j j j j j j j j

g g g g g g g g g g g g g g g g g g g g g g
g g g g g g g g g g g g g g g g g g g g g
g g g g g g g g g g g g g g g g g g g g g

4

Checklist
Sit up straight ☐
Don't grip your pen too tightly ☐
Keep your writing forearm on the desk ☐

y y y y y y y y y y y y y y y y y y y y y
y y y y y y y y y y y y y y y y y
z z z z z z z z z z z z z z z z z z z
z z z z z z z z z z z z z z z z z z z
f f f f f f f f f f f f f f f f f f f
f f f f f f f f f f f f f f f f f f f
r r r r r r r r r r r r r r r r r r r
r r r r r r r r r r r r r r r r r r r
s s s s s s s s s s s s s s s s s s s
s s s s s s s s s s s s s s s s s s s
v v v v v v v v v v v v v v v v v v v
v v v v v v v v v v v v v v v v v v v
w w w w w w w w w w w w w w w w w w w
w w w w w w w w w w w w w w w w w w w
p p p p p p p p p p p p p p p p p p p
p p p p p p p p p p p p p p p p p p p
a a a a a a a a a a a a a a a a a a a a a
a a a a a a a a a a a a a a a a a a a
a a a a a a a a a a a a a a a a a a a

CDEIMNOQI

C C C C C C C C C C C C C C C C C
C C C C C C C C C C C C C C C C C

D D D D D D D D D D D D D D D D D
D D D D D D D D D D D D D D D D D

E E E E E E E E E E E E E E E E E
E E E E E E E E E E E E E E E E E

g g g g g g g g g g g g g g g g g
g g g g g g g g g g g g g g g g g

M M M M M M M M M M M M M M M M M
M M M M M M M M M M M M M M M M M

N N N N N N N N N N N N N N N N N
N N N N N N N N N N N N N N N N N

O O O O O O O O O O O O O O O O O
O O O O O O O O O O O O O O O O O

Q Q Q Q Q Q Q Q Q Q Q Q Q Q Q Q Q
Q Q Q Q Q Q Q Q Q Q Q Q Q Q Q Q Q

I I I I I I I I I I I I I I I I I
I I I I I I I I I I I I I I I I I
I I I I I I I I I I I I I I I I I

𝒰 𝒳 𝒴 𝒵 ℱ ℛ 𝒮 𝒰 𝒲

𝒰 𝒰 𝒰 𝒰 𝒰 𝒰 𝒰 𝒰 𝒰 𝒰 𝒰 𝒰 𝒰 𝒰 𝒰 𝒰 𝒰

𝓊 𝓊 𝓊 𝓊 𝓊 𝓊 𝓊 𝓊 𝓊 𝓊 𝓊 𝓊 𝓊 𝓊 𝓊

𝒳 𝒳 𝒳 𝒳 𝒳 𝒳 𝒳 𝒳 𝒳 𝒳 𝒳 𝒳 𝒳 𝒳 𝒳 𝒳

𝓍 𝓍 𝓍 𝓍 𝓍 𝓍 𝓍 𝓍 𝓍 𝓍 𝓍 𝓍 𝓍 𝓍 𝓍 𝓍

𝒴 𝒴 𝒴 𝒴 𝒴 𝒴 𝒴 𝒴 𝒴 𝒴 𝒴 𝒴 𝒴 𝒴 𝒴 𝒴

𝓎 𝓎 𝓎 𝓎 𝓎 𝓎 𝓎 𝓎 𝓎 𝓎 𝓎 𝓎 𝓎 𝓎 𝓎 𝓎

𝒵 𝒵 𝒵 𝒵 𝒵 𝒵 𝒵 𝒵 𝒵 𝒵 𝒵 𝒵 𝒵 𝒵 𝒵 𝒵

𝓏 𝓏 𝓏 𝓏 𝓏 𝓏 𝓏 𝓏 𝓏 𝓏 𝓏 𝓏 𝓏

ℱ ℱ ℱ ℱ ℱ ℱ ℱ ℱ ℱ ℱ ℱ ℱ ℱ ℱ ℱ ℱ ℱ

𝓎 𝓎 𝓎 𝓎 𝓎 𝓎 𝓎 𝓎 𝓎 𝓎 𝓎 𝓎 𝓎 𝓎 𝓎 𝓎

ℛ ℛ ℛ ℛ ℛ ℛ ℛ ℛ ℛ ℛ ℛ ℛ ℛ ℛ ℛ ℛ

𝓀 𝓀 𝓀 𝓀 𝓀 𝓀 𝓀 𝓀 𝓀 𝓀 𝓀 𝓀 𝓀 𝓀

𝒮 𝒮 𝒮 𝒮 𝒮 𝒮 𝒮 𝒮 𝒮 𝒮 𝒮 𝒮 𝒮 𝒮 𝒮 𝒮

𝓈 𝓈 𝓈 𝓈 𝓈 𝓈 𝓈 𝓈 𝓈 𝓈 𝓈 𝓈 𝓈 𝓈 𝓈 𝓈

𝒰 𝒰 𝒰 𝒰 𝒰 𝒰 𝒰 𝒰 𝒰 𝒰 𝒰 𝒰 𝒰 𝒰 𝒰 𝒰

𝓋 𝓋 𝓋 𝓋 𝓋 𝓋 𝓋 𝓋 𝓋 𝓋 𝓋 𝓋 𝓋 𝓋 𝓋 𝓋

𝒲 𝒲 𝒲 𝒲 𝒲 𝒲 𝒲 𝒲 𝒲 𝒲 𝒲 𝒲 𝒲 𝒲 𝒲 𝒲

𝓌 𝓌 𝓌 𝓌 𝓌 𝓌 𝓌 𝓌 𝓌 𝓌 𝓌 𝓌 𝓌 𝓌 𝓌

𝓌 𝓌 𝓌 𝓌 𝓌 𝓌 𝓌 𝓌 𝓌 𝓌 𝓌 𝓌 𝓌 𝓌 𝓌 𝓌

Checklist
Sit up straight ☐
Don't grip your pen too tightly ☐
Keep your writing forearm on the desk ☐

p p p p p p p p p p p p p p p p p p p p p p p p p p p p
p p p p p p p p p p p p p p p p p p p p p p p p p p p p

acde acde acde acde acde acde acde

imno imno imno imno imno imno imno

hkll hkll hkll hkll hkll hkll hkll

qtux qtux qtux qlux qlux qlux qlux

jgyz jgyz jgyz jgyz jgyz jgyz

frs frs frs frs frs frs frs frs frs

vwp vwp uwp uwp uwp uwp uwp

dth dth dth dth dth dth dth dth

ACD ACD ACD ACD ACD ACD

EIM EIM EIM EIM EIM EIM

NOQ NOQ NOQ NOQ NOQ NOQ

TUX TUX TUX TUX TUX TUX

HKL HKL HKL HKL HKL HKL

BGY BGY BGY BGY BGY BGY

YZF YZF YZF YZF YZF YZF

RSV RSV RSV RSV RSV RSV

WP WP WP WP WP WP WP

It Happened

b, f, h, k and !
touch the top
red line.

A rogue cow escaped from a mart in Ennis,
Co. Clare. She was dangerously out of control.
After she escaped she careered down a busy
street. A garda who tried to corral her was
knocked to the ground and dragged along.
Luckily he wasn't badly injured. Others who
tried to bring the cow under control also
suffered minor injuries. Eventually the cow
was herded into a field.

It Happened

A rogue cow escaped from a mart in Ennis,
Co. Clare. She was dangerously out of control.
After she escaped she careered down a busy
street. A garda who tried to corral
her was knocked to the ground and
dragged along. Luckily he wasn't badly
injured. Others who tried tried to bring
the cow under control also suffered
minor injuries. Eventually the cow
was herded into a field

Biodegradable Waste

Leftover waste from the kitchen, such as fruit and vegetable skins and green waste from the garden, is all biodegradable. It can be treated and turned into compost. There are huge benefits from treating waste in this way. The waste going into landfills is greatly reduced and there are fewer harmful greenhouse gas emissions. Biodegradable waste must be kept separate in special bins.

Biodegradable Waste

Leftoues waste from the kitchen, such as fruit and vegelable skins and green waste from the garden, is all biodegradable. It can be treated and turned into compos. There are huge benefits from treating waste in this way. The waste going into landfills rs greatly reduced and there are fewer harmful greenhouse gas emissions. Biodegradable waste must be kept separate in special bins

10

Maisie

Checklist
Sit up straight ☐
Don't grip your pen too tightly ☐
Keep your writing forearm on the desk ☐

Paul got his dog Bailey from a shelter. Because he worked away from home, Paul was aware that Bailey might be lonely. He picked Maisie, a lively young dog, to be Bailey's pal. On Paul's first day at work after Maisie's arrival, he put the dogs in the garden. A scene of destruction met him that evening. The shrubs were uprooted and the garden was destroyed, but the dogs were very happy!

Maisie

Paul got his dog Bailey from a shelter. Because he worked away from home Paul was aware that Bailey might be lonely. He picked Maisie, a lively young dog, to be Bailey's pal. On Paul's first day at work after Maisie's arrival, he put the dogs in the garden. A scene of destruction met him that evening. The shrubs were uprooted and the garden was destroyed, but the dogs were very happy!

11

It Happened

Loops cross at the top blue line.

A fire in a landfill in Co. Kildare burned for weeks. It was an underground fire, burning 30 metres below the surface. Plumes of acrid smoke billowed above it. Local people worried about the health risks to their families. The fire was difficult to extinguish. Extra firefighters had to be drafted in. The waste on top had to be removed before the fire could be completely put out.

It Happened

A fire in a land fill in Co. Kildare burned for weeks. It was an underground fire, burning 30 metres below the surface

'Un' Words

unabashed, unable, unacceptable, unaffected,

unanimous, unapologetic, unappetising,

unapproachable, unashamed, unavailable,

unbearable, unbelievable, unbreakable,

unburden, uncanny, unceasing, uncoil,

unconditional, unconscious, uncontested,

uncooperative, undecided, undecipherable,

undefeated, undemonstrative, undeniable,

uneducated, unemployed, unfortunate, unjust

Un Words

A Legend

In ancient times a sword suddenly appeared stuck in a stone in the centre of a town in England. A message on the sword said that whoever managed to pull it out would be crowned king. Knights travelled from far and near but none succeeded in extracting the sword. During a jousting competition in the town, a youth named Arthur pulled it out and was crowned king.

A legend

Proverbs

A bird in the hand is worth two in the bush.

A chain is only as strong as its weakest link.

A house divided against itself cannot stand.

A little knowledge is a dangerous thing.

Absolute power corrupts absolutely.

Birds of a feather flock together.

Burn the candle at both ends.

Don't look a gift horse in the mouth.

Don't keep a dog and bark yourself.

Proverbs

It Should Be Easy

'How many flowers?' asked Teacher, holding a large sunflower in each hand. 'One and one', answered Annie. 'How many altogether?' Teacher continued. 'Two', said Annie. The lesson continued. Annie counted, added and answered, two and two, three and two... 'Well done Annie', said Teacher. 'Last one for today'. She held up three and three. Annie thought hard, smiled and said, 'Loads and loads!'

Rain

Capital R joins to the next letter. F, I, T and W do not.

Rain falls on land and water. The sun heats the earth's surface. Water evaporates when it is heated. It rises into the atmosphere. It cools as it rises, condensing to form clouds and raindrops. The rain then falls to the ground. This is called the rain cycle. Too much or too little rain causes devastating floods or drought. Floods and drought cause great hardship for people and animals.

Rain

Long Ago

Capitals C and A join to the next letter. I, O, P, and T do not.

Checklist
Sit up straight ☐
Don't grip your pen too tightly ☐
Keep your writing forearm on the desk ☐

It was always cold in the classroom from October to April. There was no central heating in those days. Classrooms were huge and draughty. There was a black stove at the top of the room. Pupils brought in a sod of turf or a block of wood for the stove. If the fuel was damp it didn't give out much heat. Pupils brought milk in glass bottles and left them by the stove to warm the milk.

Long

Similes

Capital A joins to the next letter.

As bald as a coot, as black as a sweep, as blind as a bat, as bold as brass, as brave as a lion, as bright as a new pin, as busy as a bee, as clear as a bell, as clean as a whistle, as dry as dust, as dull as dishwater, as flat as a pancake, as free as a bird, as fresh as a daisy, as good as gold, as happy as a lark, as hungry as a wolf, as large as life, as old as the hills, as plain as day, as pure as snow.

Similes

Clean Up

Capital T and I do not join to the next letter.

Checklist
Sit up straight ☐
Don't grip your pen too tightly ☐
Keep your writing forearm on the desk ☐

There is an abundance of rubbish in space. It poses a serious threat to satellites. A collision in space could set off a chain reaction resulting in a threat to our communications network. A Japanese company has made a net which they hope will scoop up all the rubbish. The net and its contents will be guided back to earth and will burn up on entering the atmosphere.

Clean

Lake Monster

Cross 't' and dot 'i' when you finish a word.

Prince Fergus went swimming in a deep lake. The monster, who lived in the lake, rose in fury from the depths. Such was his size he turned the calm water into a whirlpool. He struck Fergus with his tail, leaving a big gash from his brow to his neck. The wound persisted. Fergus was given a pair of magic shoes to walk on water and fight the monster. He won the battle and was cured.

Lake

A Letter

Canal Cottage,
Sallins,
Co. Kildare.
2nd April 2012

Dear Aunt Kath,

This is a reminder of my confirmation. As my sponsor you must be in the church with me before 11.00 a.m. on May 30 th.

Lots of love.

A Letter

Earthquakes

These letters have loops: f, g, j, y and z.

Earthquakes happen along fault lines. The centre of an earthquake is called the epi-centre. Most damage is caused at the epi-centre. The worst devastation occurs in less developed countries. Buildings collapse, with great loss of life. Earthquakes are measured on the Richter scale. A minor quake measures less than three. A quake over eight is a cat-astrophe. Undersea quakes cause tsunamis.

Earthquakes

Homonyms

Loops on f, g, j, y and z cross on the lower blue line.

Checklist
Sit up straight ☐
Don't grip your pen too tightly ☐
Keep your writing forearm on the desk ☐

aid aide, allowed aloud, be bee, beach beech, board bored, bridal bridle, clause claws, coarse course, canon cannon, canter cantor, creak creek, die dye, discussed disgust, finish Finnish, gate gait, guessed guest, hall haul, have halve, jam jamb, lays laze, lessen lesson, mail male, manner manor, none nun, oar ore, pray prey, paced paste, read reed.

Homonyms

A Legend

Notice that you are writing on blue lines only: No red lines! Numbers are the same size as capital letters, e.g., May 3.

Oisín was a brave warrior. One day a horse and rider emerged from a rainbow. The rider was Niamh. She asked him to marry her and live with her in Tír na nÓg. Dazzled by her beauty, Oisín agreed. He loved Tír na nÓg but he missed his family and friends. Niamh lent him her magic horse to visit his home, warning him not to dismount. Alas, he did, turning into a wizened 300-year-old man.

A Poem

Checklist
Sit up straight ☐
Don't grip your pen too tightly ☐
Keep your writing forearm on the desk ☐

My teacher wasn't half as nice as yours seems to be. His name was Mister Unsworth and he taught us history. And when you didn't know a date he'd get you by the ear And start to twist while you sat there quite paralysed with fear. He'd twist and twist and twist your ear and twist it more and more.

a

Until at last the ear came off
and landed on the floor.
Our class was full of one-eared boys.
I'm certain there were eight.
Who'd had them twisted off because
they didn't know a date.
So let us now praise teachers who today
are all so fine.
And yours in particular is totally divine.

Until

It Happened

A curious pig left a farm and wandered onto the extremely busy Headford road near Galway. Traffic screeched to a halt. Shocked motorists honked their horns, hoping to scare the pig off the busy road. The pig was oblivious to the chaos. One driver tried to drive the pig onto the grass verge. The pig chased him! His embarrassed owner arrived and managed to capture him.

First Names

o, v, w, and b finish with a 'curved' line.

Aaron, Amy, Ann, Ben, Beth, Brigid, Cathal,
Craig, Daisy, David, Douglas, Eanna, Ella,
Eoin, Fionn, Flora, Frances, Gerard, Grace,
Gwen, Hilary, Hope, Iseult, Ivan, James, Jane,
John, Jude, Kathleen, Keith, Laura, Lawrence,
Mandy, Maura, Michael, Neil, Norman,
Nuala, Oliver, Olivia, Patricia, Paul, Peter,
Richard, Roberta, Ron, Sarah, Shane, Seán,
Tara, Thomas, Tony, Ursula, Valerie, Vincent.

First

 'Ex' Words

Loops on b, h and l cross on the top blue line.

Checklist
Sit up straight ☐
Don't grip your pen too tightly ☐
Keep your writing forearm on the desk ☐

exaggerate. examination. examine. example.
excavate. excellence. executive. exemplary.
exempt. exhaustion. exhibition. exhilarate.
existence. exodus. exonerate. exorbitant. expanse.
expatriate. explanation. explicable. expensive.
experience. expertise. exploit. explosion.
exposure. expulsion. expunge. exquisite.
extenuate. external. extraction. extraordinary.
extravagant. exuberant. exultant. extrapolate.

'Ex'

Characteristics

Loops cross at the top blue line.

big, small, tall, short, fat, thin, chubby, stocky, fair, dark, blonde, bald, young, old, middle-aged, kind, cruel, helpful, clever, stupid, intelligent, articulate, optimistic, pessimistic, hopeful, generous, mean, extravagant, gregarious, pretentious, anxious, laid back, talented, funny, happy, sad, lonely, lazy, amusing, frightened, excited, fearful, outgoing, diligent, neat, tidy, messy, cheerful, smiling.

Characteristics

Long Ago

r and s go slightly above the top blue line.

Checklist
Sit up straight ☐
Don't grip your pen too tightly ☐
Keep your writing forearm on the desk ☐

There was little art taught in school long ago. Classes were much bigger, often with over 50 pupils, so there wouldn't have been room. Girls learnt knitting, sewing, tacking, running and hemming. They learnt how to make buttonholes, pleats and gathers. A special copy was kept with samples of the work. Every year an inspector visited to examine the work. Boys were taught to knit as well.

Long

Group Words

The space between words is the width of a small 'o'.

A herd of hippopotami, a parcel of hogs, a stable of horses, a pack of hounds, a smack of jellyfish, a mob of kangaroos, an exaltation of larks, a leap of leopards, a pride of lions, a lounge of lizards, a herd of llamas, a plague of locusts, a horde of mice, a tribe of monkeys, a pack of mules, a parliament of owls, a drove of oxen, a bed of oysters, a muster of peacocks, a parcel of penguins.

Group

'In' Words

inability, inaccessible, inane, inanimate, inarticulate, incessant, incinerate, incision, inclement, inclusive, incognito, incompetent, inconceivable, incur, inconspicuous, inconvenient, incorrigible, incredible, indebted, indecisive, indelible, independent, indicative, indifferent, indignation, indirect, indiscriminate, inept, indolent, ineffective, ineligible, inertia, infallible, inferior, infiltrate,

Snow

Checklist

Sit up straight ☐

Don't grip your pen too tightly ☐

Keep your writing forearm on the desk ☐

Snow can have a drastic effect on everyday life. Temperatures are often dangerously low. Travelling becomes extremely difficult. Public transport often grinds to a halt. Schools close and airports cannot function unless runways are kept clear and planes de-iced. The old and the very young are at risk of hypothermia. It is essential to care for them and keep them warm and cosy.

Snow

The Bermuda Triangle

The Bermuda Triangle is in the western part of the North Atlantic Ocean. In 1945 a bomber plane disappeared in this area. To add to the mystery, a search and rescue plane dispatched to the area disappeared too. There are reports of other planes and ships that vanished mysteriously as well. Some say there are natural explanations for these incidents. Others disagree. Who knows?

The

Riddles

Notice that you are writing on 'copy' lines.

Why were the chickens ordered to leave the farm?
What's small and cuddly and bright purple?
What happens when a cat eats a lemon?
What's the difference between an injured lion and a wet day?
What did one tomato say to the other?
What's worse than finding a worm in your apple?
Why do golfers carry an extra pair of socks?
Why did the police wake the child?
What is the longest word in the English language?
The more you have of it, the less you see of it. What is it?
What has to be broken before you can use it?
How many bricks does it take to complete a brick wall?
What question can you never honestly answer 'yes' to?

Riddles

Answers

Because they used fowl language.

A koala bear holding its breath.

It becomes a sour puss.

One pours with rain and the other roars with pain.

'You go ahead and I'll ketchup.'

Finding half a worm in your apple.

In case they get a hole in one.

Because they heard there had been a kidnapping.

Smiles – because there is a mile between s and s.

Darkness.

An egg.

Only one – the last one.

Are you asleep?

Answers

Compound Words

Shortbread, handcuff, waistline, teapot, bedclothes, wallpaper, comeback, sheepskin, tableware, warehouse, telltale, teaspoon, upmarket, backlash, goodbye, jackpot, fishmonger, nutcracker, newsletter, backstroke, scarecrow, wayfarer, overboard, eardrum, jellybean, postcard, earache, motorcycle, doorstep, waylaid, nightfall, deadend, wayside, eggshell, limelight, haircut, stopwatch, earring, housework, sunglasses, turntable, forewarn, horseman, moonlit, foregone, rainwater, catwalk, timetable, starfish, lukewarm, grasshopper, underground, honeydew, toothpaste, diskdrive, upheld, headquarters, supersonic, watchdog, forehead, backlog, forecast, bookmark, forklift, eyesight, textbook, brainwave, friendship, standby, storeroom, grandstand, forbid, upstart, carefree.

Compound

Occupations

Checklist
Sit up straight ☐
Don't grip your pen too tightly ☐
Keep your writing forearm on the desk ☐

An accountant keeps or inspects financial records.
A blacksmith makes and repairs iron things by hand.
A comedian is an entertainer who makes people laugh.
A detective investigates crimes.
A fishmonger sells fish.
A geologist deals with the physical structure of the earth.
A milliner designs and makes hats.
An inventor creates something new.
A jeweller designs, makes and sells jewellery.
A lawyer studies and practises law.
A newscaster reads the news on radio or television.
An ornithologist studies birds.
A treasurer manages the finances of a company.

Occupations

Counting Chickens

One day a young milkmaid carried a large jug of milk to market. As she walked along she daydreamed. She imagined the amount of money she would get for the milk. With that money she would buy baby chicks. When they were grown she would sell them and buy kids. She would get good money for them when they were fully grown goats. Now she could afford to buy another cow. With two cows she could make twice as much money selling milk. In her imagination her fortune kept growing. She even visualised the cottage she would live in one day. Unfortunately she was so engrossed in her daydream she didn't see the root of a tree stretched across her path. She tripped over it. fell and watched in dismay as the milk soaked away.

Counting

Group Words

A troupe of acrobats, a team of athletes, a babble of barbers, a board of directors, a staff of employees, a panel of experts, a melody of harpists, a gang of hoodlums, a bench of judges, a cavalcade of horsemen, a bevy of ladies, an eloquence of lawyers, an audience of listeners, an illusion of magicians, an orchestra of musicians, a tribe of natives, a crowd of onlookers, a posse of police, a band of robbers, a crew of sailors, a house of senators, a choir of singers, a den of thieves, a flock of tourists, a coven of witches, a worship of writers, a picket of strikers, a class of students, an absence of waiters, an amble of walkers, an ambush of widows, a congregation of worshippers, a creche of youngsters, a cacophony of youths.

Group

A Legend

Checklist

Sit up straight ☐

Don't grip your pen too tightly ☐

Keep your writing forearm on the desk ☐

Once upon a time a miser hid his gold. He searched long and hard for a good hiding place. He dug a hole under a tree in his garden and buried the gold there. Once a week, in the middle of the night, he dug up his treasure. He gloated over it, rubbed his hands in delight and buried it again. Word of his behaviour spread. A thief watched him, waited until it was safe, dug up the gold and fled with it. When the miser discovered his gold was stolen he raised a commotion. His neighbours came running to see what was amiss. He told them what had happened. 'Did you ever spend any gold?' asked one man. 'Of course not,' answered the miser. 'I just looked at it.' 'Well then,' said the man, 'Just look at the empty hole. It'll be just as good!'

a

Tongue Twisters

I saw a saw that could outsaw any saw I ever saw.

Tricky tongue twisters trip thrillingly off the tongue.

Six slippery snails slid slowly seaward.

A noisy noise annoys an oyster.

Round and round the rugged rock the ragged rascal ran.

Twelve twins twirled twelve twigs.

If you notice this notice, you will notice this notice is not worth noticing.

Eleven owls licked eleven little liquorice lollipops.

Zero zebra zigzagged into the zoo.

Five frantic frogs fled from fifty fierce fish.

Bake big batches of brown blueberry bread.

There was a minimum of cinnamon in the aluminium pan.

Tongue

Words Ending in 'ist'

activist, antagonist, artist, assist, atheist, backlist, bassoonist, bicyclist, biologist, botanist, canoeist, catechist, cardiologist, checklist, chemist, chiropodist, columnist, consist, copyist, dentist, desist, dramatist, elitist, enlist, escapist, exist, extremist, fantasist, fist, florist, foist, geologist, gemologist, gist, guitarist, handlist, harpist, heist, herbalist, idealist, industrialist, insist, joist, journalist, linguist, list, lutist, machinist, motorist, motorcyclist, neurologist, novelist, optimist, pessimist, pharmacist, pianist, realist, scientist, shortlist, stylist, tatooist, terrorist, therapist, twist, unionist, untwist, ventriloquist, verbalist, violinist, vocalist, vocationalist, vulcanologist, waist, whist, wrist, xylophonist, zoologist.

Words

Eyjafjallojokull

In 2010 Eyjafjallojokull erupted in Iceland. The force of the eruption caused torrents of lava to burst through the ice sheet and sent clouds of ash billowing high into the sky. Prevailing winds blew the huge ash cloud across the Atlantic Ocean towards Europe. The eruption lasted for months and had devastating effects on air travel throughout the continent. Volcanic ash is extremely abrasive and can destroy aircraft engines. For safety, vast areas of airspace were closed to flights and the travel arrangements of millions of people were severely disrupted. Many were stranded far from home with little money and no accommodation. With such large numbers trying to get home, buses, trains and ferries did good business.

Eyjafjallojokull

Unusual Pets

It has become fashionable to keep a pig as a pet. These pigs are not the farmyard pigs we are used to. Pot-bellied pigs are a different breed. They are highly intelligent and can be both leash and house trained. They are affectionate, playful and curious. However, they can be headstrong and sensitive. Unless entertained and stimulated they will become bored and destructive. They constantly look for food and can learn to open cupboards and fridges. At mealtimes they beg for food and can become aggressive if denied. The micro pig is tiny when born - the size of a cup. The adult is just over one foot long. They are very clean, they love company and will even play with toys but like nothing better than having their bellies scratched!

Unusual

The Last Day

He just couldn't believe it. He had spent the last eight years in this school. He knew its every nook and cranny. It held many memories for him – most of them good. He could recall all his teachers. some wonderful. others not so wonderful. He loved so many things about this school. His sporting talents had been fostered here. Being captain of the school football team was his greatest achievement. His team mates would be his friends forever. Their proudest moment was winning the county final. Luckily many of his friends were moving on to the same second-level school. It would be strange to be starting off as a junior again. He wouldn't think about that now. He set off to say good-bye to all the teachers and have them sign his shirt.

The